Professor Jim's
METEOR ADVENTURE!

It's a family night out with the stars.

Discover a new revolution in observing the earth as it moves through space.

By **PROFESSOR Jim Pressler, Ph.D.**
Reading Specialist, Astronomer

PRINTED AND PUBLISHED IN THE USA BY:
JAMES PRESSLER, BOX 813,
WHITE PIGEON, MICHIGAN, USA 49099

www.iread-edu.com
jimxpressler@yahoo.com

Second printing began in November
2015 CREATESPACE

ISBN-13: 978-0-9788828-2-2

This handbook is the third book in the reading improvement series.

Other books by **Professor Jim, Ph.D.:**

BOOK 1: **Professor Jim's**
        Beginning Reading Adventures!
        FAT CAT AT BAT! With Writing and Math.
Includes Professor Jim's Discovery of the Origin of the Alphabet.

BOOK 2: **Professor Jim's**
        Advanced Reading Adventures!
        RIMES AND SIGNS FOR SAFETY

BOOK 4: **Professor Jim's**
        Wisdom for Sages of All Ages!
        A children's epic rime
        where their dreams can pass the time.

Dedicated to...

Parents, teachers, and all who cared
With hopes & dreams and all they've shared.

Who know the benefits reading provides,
To aid their students all of their lives.

Preventing reading troubles and strife,
And command the greatest time of their life.

They hone many child's talent and skill,
So their dreams and ideas can become real.

HELPFUL HINTS FOR PARENTS AND EDUCATORS

The first part of this book is designed for early readers. It is written in all upper case style of print, which reduces confusion of the letter shapes. Most books are written in mixed case, which can be confusing when learning to read. This book then advances to mixed case, for advanced readers.

When reading along with children, slow down occasionally at simple three or four letter words and sound each symbol as your child or student points to each symbol. This will help a new reader understand that our reading system is based on a sound for a symbol relationship. A child must see the symbols as they hear the sounds.

Reading is simply turning these written symbols back into spoken words. Reading is the foundation of learning.

Children can be drilled to memorize thousands of words, but if they do not know the next word, they cannot read it. With **PROFESSOR JIM'S** method, the words will almost speak-out to the child when they understand the alphabet symbols as sounds.

A child cannot learn these sounds from a book on their own. It is a secret alphabetic code that has to be explained or taught to new or beginning readers. These sounds are the code that all readers have agreed to use for each particular symbol and combination of symbols.

With **PROFESSOR JIM'S** method, you can teach children in a few minutes or hours, things that could take weeks, years, or a lifetime, for them to learn on their own.

This book is for all ages and reading levels. It starts simply and each chapter gradually builds to include more advanced readers.

Parents and educators can enjoy giving their children the greatest gift,—the ability to read.

Individualize this handbook by placing your child or student's name in upper case symbols on the front cover, or on a separate sheet of paper. Students can trace over their name as they associate the sounds with each symbol in their name.

STARS ON EACH PAGE

This handbook can be used to record a reader's progress. A student is to receive a star for each page they read. Children can see immediate accomplishment and this gives them a sense of their individual achievement as they become involved in reading. The star can be a sticker, a star marker pen, or simply drawn on a numbered sheet of paper.

This practice provides early readers with ownership, and gives them a reward incentive to be motivated and involved in their reading. Parents and educators can also see immediate improvements and individual progress.

MISSION STATEMENT

Our mission is to inspire people to read with excellence and to better understand the world and the cosmos. We hope this book helps inspire your child or student to succeed in life and to help them make their hopes and dreams become reality.

ACKNOWLEDGMENTS

Dedicated to our parents, grandparents, and ancestors, as well as to our children and grandchildren, and future descendants.

My three sons, Marcus, Travis, and Alexander, put me in the chain of life and inspired me to feel the success of reading with excellence, and to teach others.

I would like to thank the best students in the world, my students at the *iREAD ACADEMY* who gave me years of experience, enlightenment, and satisfaction.

PROFESSOR JIM PRESSLER Ph.D.

CONTENTS

PART ONE

This book is designed to build a readers confidence, and reading ability. It starts out easy for early readers then the chapters progressively increase in difficulty.

PART ONE
FOR EARLY READERS

CHAPTER		PAGE
I	*THE ADVENTURE BEGINS!*	1
	For beginning readers.	
II	*AND AWAY WE GO!*	9
	For early readers	
III	*THE MYSTERY OF THE UNIVERSE REVEALED*	13
	For young readers	
IV	*THE GREAT ORION ASCENDING*	21
	Mixed case symbols. For middle grade readers.	
V	*BIRTHDAY SURPRISE!*	24
VI	*ASTEROIDS, COMETS, AND METEORS, OH MY!*	26
VII	*THE FIREFLY ENCOUNTER*	28
VIII	*THE CAMPSITE ARRIVAL*	31
IX	*EARTHLINGS TRAVEL AT FANTASTIC SPEED*	35
X	*GRAB YOUR SEAT AS YOU WATCH THE EARTH MOVE!*	37

PART TWO
FOR ADVANCED READERS

XI	*FOR PRESENT AND FUTURE ASTRONOMERS, ASTROPHYSICISTS, AND STAR GAZERS!*	45
XII	*DISASTER*	47
XIII	*SPEEDING THROUGH SPACE*	48
XIV	*MAJOR METEOR SHOWERS*	55
XV	*RECORD YOUR METEOR SHOWER ACTIVITY*	58

About the Author and Illustrator

Examples of the first two books in:
Professor Jim's READING ADVENTURES

PART ONE

FOR BEGINNING AND YOUNG READERS

2

CHAPTER 1

THE ADVENTURE BEGINS!

IT WAS A COOL AND STARRY NIGHT, AS THE OLD STEAM TRAIN PULLED INTO THE STATION.

PROFESSOR JIM, HIS WIFE, THE TWINS ALEX AND ALEXIA, AND A DOG NAMED CABOOSE, WERE EXCITED TO GO ON A CAMPING TRIP METEOR ADVENTURE.

THE FAMILY WAS ABOUT TO SEE ONE OF NATURES MOST AMAZING SPECTACLES —THE EARTH AS IT TRAVELS THROUGH SPACE ON ITS TRIP AROUND THE SUN.

WHEN YOU WATCH A METEOR SHOWER, IT IS THE ONLY EVENT WHEN YOU CAN ACTUALLY SEE AND EXPERIENCE THE INCREDIBLE SPEED AND DIRECTION THE EARTH IS TRAVELING!

TOOT,
TOOT,
TOOT, WENT THE WHISTLE,
SCREEEEEEECH,
HISSSSSSSSSS,
AND A BIG PUFF
OF STEAM AS
THE TRAIN
CAME TO A STOP.

"WE ARE ALMOST THERE!"
EXCLAIMED PROFESSOR JIM.

"WOW, RIDING ON A TRAIN
IS FUN!" ALEX CHEERED.

"I CAN HARDLY WAIT TO SEE THE METEOR SHOWER," ALEXIA SQUEALED WITH DELIGHT.

"BOW-WOW," BARKED CABOOSE.

ALEX KNEW THAT A METEOR WAS A STREAK OF LIGHT THAT LEAVES A TRAIL ACROSS THE NIGHT SKY, BUT HE WASN'T SURE WHAT A METEOR SHOWER WAS. HE ASKED, "WHAT EXACTLY IS A METEOR SHOWER, MOM?"

MOM EXPLAINED, "IT IS CALLED A METEOR SHOWER BECAUSE ON CERTAIN DAYS OF THE YEAR, THE NUMBER OF METEORS INCREASE.

AS THEY EXITED THE TRAIN, MOM CHECKED ALL THEIR CAMPING GEAR. THE CHAIRS WERE FOR RELAXING WHILE VIEWING THE METEORS.

PROFESSOR JIM ADDED, "WHEN A COMET OR ASTEROID PASSES NEAR THE SUN IT LEAVES A TRAIL OF DUST BEHIND.

WE CAN SEE METEOR SHOWERS ONLY FROM ABOUT MIDNIGHT UNTIL MORNING DAYBREAK. THAT IS WHEN OUR LOCATION PLUNGES INTO THE COMET'S DUST TRAIL.

METEOR SHOWERS ARE MYSTERIOUS BECAUSE NO ONE KNOWS EXACTLY HOW MANY METEORS WILL FALL. THEY ARE DAZZLING AND FREE; THEY CAN BE SEEN WITHOUT USING A TELESCOPE OR ANY SPECIAL EQUIPMENT."

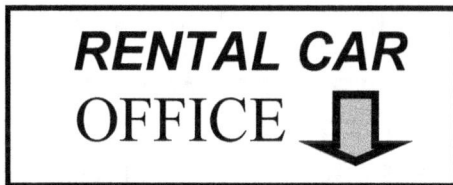

RENTAL CAR
OFFICE ⬇

AS THEY WALKED TO THE RENTAL CAR OFFICE, ALEXIA LOOKED UP AT THE GLITTERING SKY SPRINKLED WITH STARS, "LOOK AT ALL THOSE STARS!" SHE SIGHED.

"THE SKY IS SO CLEAR... WAY OUT HERE AWAY FROM THE CITY LIGHTS. IT LOOKS LIKE I COULD REACH UP AND CATCH A FALLING STAR."

"—AND PUT IT IN YOUR POCKET," MOM HUMMED A TUNE FROM MEMORY AS SHE HELD BACK A LAUGH, "IT'S AN OLD SONG...SORRY."

AS THE PROFESSOR RENTED A CAR, HE SAID, "ONE OF MY EARLIEST MEMORIES WAS OF MY BROTHER AND I LAYING IN THE GRASS AT NIGHT WITH STARS THAT SPARKLED LIKE DIAMONDS, AS HE TOLD ME ABOUT THE HEAVENS."

"I WANT TO BE AN ASTRONOMER," ALEXIA SAID WITH IMAGINATION.

"YOU ARE ALREADY AN ASTRONOMER," MOM EXPLAINED. ASTRO IS FOR A STAR. NOMEN IS FOR NAMING OR NUMBERING. AN ASTRONOMER IS A PERSON WHO STUDIES THE STARS. THAT IS WHAT WE ARE DOING."

MOM CONTINUED, "DID YOU KNOW THE BEST BEGINNING SCIENTISTS ARE CHILDREN?"

"OH REALLY? I THOUGHT ONLY OLD PEOPLE WERE SCIENTISTS," SAID ALEXIA.

MOM REPLIED, "AS A RULE, CHILDREN MAKE THE BEST SCIENTISTS. THEY FEEL FREE TO INVESTIGATE AND EXPLORE THE WORLD WITH A FRESH NEW OUTLOOK. BUT, AND THIS IS A VERY BIG BUT, CHILDREN NEED THE TOOLS OF A GOOD EDUCATION IN THIS INFORMATION AGE. THEY NEED TO READ AND WRITE WITH EXCELLENCE, CONFIDENCE AND UNDERSTANDING."

THE PROFESSOR SMILED AND NODDED IN AGREEMENT, "IT'S GOOD TO LEARN THE PREFIXES, ROOTS, AND SUFFIXES. THEY CAN HELP YOU LEARN THOUSANDS OF WORDS IN A MATTER OF MINUTES.

WHO IS IN CHARGE OF YOUR LEARNING? ... NOT YOUR TEACHERS... NOT ME—YES, IT IS YOU. NO ONE CAN MAKE YOU LEARN. WITH GOOD READING SKILLS YOU CAN LEARN FROM THE GREATEST MINDS THROUGHOUT HISTORY, AND THIS CAN CHANGE YOUR LIFE FOR THE BETTER."

"I DIDN'T KNOW I WAS A SCIENTIST! I DO LIKE TO FIGURE STUFF OUT." REMARKED ALEX.

MOM ADJUSTED THE CAR SEAT, "CHILDREN ARE NATURAL GENIUSES— CURIOUS, COURAGEOUS, AND ADVENTUROUS. NO ONE KNOWS WHAT WILL CAPTURE A CHILD'S IMAGINATION. NO ONE HAS TOLD THEM THAT IT, "CAN'T-BE-DONE," AS MOM RAISED HER TWO HANDS UP AND MADE QUOTE MARKS IN THE AIR.

THE PROFESSOR STRAIGHTENED HIS HAT, "SCIENTISTS, PHILOSOPHERS, AND GREAT THINKERS DO NOT JUST BECOME THAT WAY AS AN ADULT. THEIR INTEREST AND PASSION DEVELOPED FROM THEIR CURIOSITY, EDUCATION, AND MOTIVATION AS A CHILD."

THE TWINS READ THE SIGN:

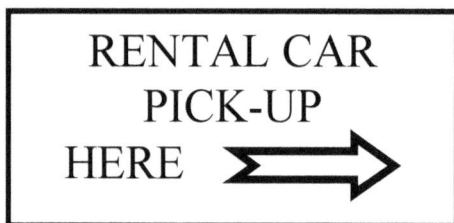

RENTAL CAR
PICK-UP
HERE ⟹

CHAPTER 2

AND AWAY WE GO!

AS THEY LOADED THEIR COOLER, SLEEPING BAGS, AND GEAR INTO THEIR NEW RENTAL CAR, THE PROFESSOR HOPPED BEHIND THE WHEEL. "IS *EVERYBODY* READY?—THEN OFF WE GO!" HE SQUEALED THE TIRES AS THEY EXITED THE PARKING LOT.

"DAD!" THE TWINS YELLED AS ONE.

"WE'RE ALL GONNA DIE!" SQUEALED ALEXIA AS THE CHILDREN LAUGHED AT DAD'S ACTIONS.

"I'M NOT USED TO THIS GAS PEDAL!" THE PROFESSOR TRIED TO DOWN-PLAY HIS RUN-IN.

"YEAH, RIGHT, SURE," MOM AGREED A LITTLE TOO WILLINGLY, AS THE PROFESSOR RAISED HIS EYEBROWS.

"EASY DAD, JUST 'CAUSE IT'S A RENTAL..." ALEX CHIDED.

"RUFF, RUFF," BARKED CABOOSE AS HE HUNG HIS HEAD DOWN OVER THE FRONT SEAT AND WHINED.

THE MOONLIGHT SHONE BRIGHTLY ON MOM'S YOUNG FACE. SHE TOOK ON A FAR-OFF LOOK, AS SHE LOOKED OUT THE WINDOW, "WE ARE ALL CHILDREN WHEN WE LOOK UP AT THE HEAVENS AND MARVEL AT THE MYSTERY OF THE STARS. YOU CAN THANK YOUR LUCKY STARS THAT YOUR DAD AND I HAVE GIVEN YOU THE MIRACLE OF LIFE. YOU HAVE BEEN BORN INTO THE GREATEST RACE IN THE UNIVERSE—THE HUMAN RACE.

ALL HUMANS HAVE THE SAME GENES—"

"YOU MEAN LIKE THE SAME KIND OF BLUE JEANS?" ALEX GIGGLED AS HE CUT IN, KNOWING THAT HE WAS INTERRUPTING.

MOM CONTINUED, "WE ARE ALL ONE FAMILY OF BROTHERS AND SISTERS—THE SAME GENETICS AS EACH OTHER.

WE ARE TRAVELING TOGETHER ON THIS ADVENTURE BY CAR. THIS IS SIMILAR TO ALL PEOPLE ON PLANET EARTH. WE ARE TRAVELING THROUGH SPACE IN A GALAXY OF STARS ON OUR COSMIC JOURNEY."

THE PROFESSOR CLEARED HIS THROAT, "WE ARE ALL SCIENTISTS AND PHILOSOPHERS THAT ARE LEARNING ABOUT OUR PART IN THE GREATEST HUMAN EXPERIMENT—CALLED HUMANITY."

"WHAT IS A PHILOSOPHER?" ASKED ALEXIA.

"A PHILOSOPHER IS SOMEONE WITH THE A LOVE OF LEARNING AND STRIVING FOR WISDOM. THEY SEEK ENLIGHTENMENT—FOR THEMSELVES AND FOR THE WORLD. PHILOS IS FOR LOVE OF; SOPHIA IS FOR LEARNING AND WISDOM," MOM REPLIED.

"WHERE DOES THE SKY START?
HOW HIGH IS THE SKY?" ASKED ALEX AS
HE LOOKED OUT THE CAR'S MOON
ROOF.

"REACH UP AS HIGH AS YOU CAN!"
YELLED THE PROFESSOR AS HE PUT HIS
ARM AND HEAD OUT THE WINDOW. THE
CHILDREN PUT THEIR HANDS OUT THE
WINDOWS INTO THE COOL NIGHT AIR.
THE SKY STARTS AT YOUR FINGERTIPS.
IT GOES PAST THE MOON, THE STARS,
AND FARTHER THAN YOU CAN IMAGINE."
HE PULLED BACK INSIDE THE CAR.

"I HAVE A GOOD IMAGINATION."
PROBED ALEX.

"YES YOU DO, BUT—AND THIS IS
ANOTHER VERY BIG BUT…" THE TWINS
GIGGLED AS THE PROFESSOR
CONTINUED, "NO PERSON HAS EVER
SEEN A LIMIT TO THE NUMBER OF STARS
OR TO THE SIZE OF OUR UNIVERSE,
EVEN WITH THE GREATEST TELESCOPES
ON EARTH AND IN SPACE…" HIS VOICE
FADED.

A RACCOON SCURRIED OFF AS THE
CAR'S HEADLIGHTS CUT THE DARKNESS.

CHAPTER 3

THE MYSTERY OF THE UNIVERSE REVEALED

Alex asked, "Why is it called the Universe?"

"The Universe is everything including the Earth, the solar system, stars, planets, and galaxies. The Universe in harmony is called the Cosmos. Uni- is for "one," verse, is for "turn into song," the Professor stated. "We all sing together."

"Thanks Dad," praised Alex. "I know you like long explanations, which helps me understand and think things over. And I love to read."

"You have grown up quickly. You can be proud and confident of yourself," said the Professor.

He thought of his years and how they had seemed to rush by.

Long explanations help to teach and prepare children for an unknown future. A child's success depends on excellence in reading, writing, and math skills. If you want to see the future, look into a child's eyes. Guide a child in expressing themselves to better communicate with others. "I have a dream job," the Professor repeats often. "I make dreams come true, through academic excellence."

"Mom, what is a star?" Asked Alexia.

"Our sun is a star," Mom answered eagerly. "It is the closest star to earth, called Sol—as in solar.

There are more stars and planets in the Universe than all the grains of sand in the world."

"That's a lot of stars...and a lot of space." Alex's voice trailed off, deep in thought.

"I would like to be a star someday," Alexia dreamed out loud.

"To be a star is an ancient Egyptian idea or philosophy. The ancient Egyptians thought we became stars after we die," Mom pointed to a random star in the cool night sky. "They believed their ancestors were the stars and actually watching over them.

Your spirit shines bright. You are the brilliant superstars of Dad and I."

Professor Jim added, "Did you know that there is a 5-pointed star inside of every apple? If you cut the apple across the center, you can see it. A 5 pointed star was the symbol for "to teach" in ancient Egypt. I think that is why we give an apple to a teacher today. Some traditions take a long time to break!"

Alexia tested Alex, "Do you know how to draw a star?"

"Yes," Alex drew on a napkin as Mom turned on the dome light, "You draw two lines like the start of the letter 'A' then another line over; across; then back down to where you started."

The Professor interrupted, "—have you heard, "An apple a day keeps the doctor away? Did you know that doctors are afraid of apples?"

"Daaaad!" Alex corrected. "That just means that apples are healthful and that you don't need a doctor!"

"Oh, I see—yes, you're probably right," conceded the Professor with a big smile. Alex smiled too. He knew that his dad was just kidding.

"How far away is the sun, Dad?" Alexia asked.

"About 150 million kilometers," Professor Jim answered. "Which is almost 93 million miles—very far.

You want to use the metric system when possible." The Professor ranted. "The metric system is far simpler and easier to use.

Mom cut in, "I grew up with both systems, and all the confusion. I hope you use the metric system... old habits are hard to break."

Professor Jim went back to explaining, "You never want to look directly at the sun, but imagine taking a high speed train speeding faster than a racecar, at 300 kilometers per hour, which is about 186 miles per hour, on a trip to the sun. It would take over 57 years to get there!

Alex chimed in, "We could travel day and night! Oh—well—no, there would be no night if we would be on our way to the sun!"

Alexia groaned, then laughed, "Ha, Alex, that's funny."

The Professor continued, "The earth goes around the sun in only 365 and one fourth days. Everything on the earth is traveling at fantastic speed, over 100 thousand kilometers per hour, which is over 66,000 miles per hour!

If the earth were to travel any slower, it would quickly spiral into the sun—not good for earthlings!"

Alex asked, "What is a planet?"

"Planets are things that go around, revolve, or orbit a sun. Mom said, "We are on one right now, the Earth. There are many other stars with planets like Earth."

Alexia spoke up confidently, "We learned in science class that we live on a Goldilocks planet. It's not too hot, or not too cold, but just right! Earth is the only place in the entire Universe where we know life exists.

If there is life out there, with our giant radio telescopes listening, we should have heard a signal by now. But the heavens are silent. If we are the only planet to have life in the Universe, how special and alone we are. If everyone knew that we are the only beings in the whole Universe, you would think we could get along with each other a little better. To have all the world wars and chaos, it is pretty dreadful—because humans really are the only sole survivors."

Alex added, "There are most likely no other civilizations. Other alien beings must have killed each other off— or never developed radio signals! When we hurt each other, we are really hurting all of our family of humankind." Then he questioned Alexia, "Do you know the planets in order?"

"Yes!" Answered Alexia. "Mercury, Venus, Earth, Mars, Jupiter, Saturn, Uranus, and Neptune.

"And the dwarf planets?"

"Yes, Ceres, Humea, Makemake, Pluto, and Eris," She quickly replied.

"Does anyone know Pallas, Juno, and Vesta?" The Professor probed. "They were called planets for many years, but are now just minor planets."

Alex admitted uneasily, "Never heard of them."

Nope, Alexia silently thought without replying.

CHAPTER 4

THE GREAT ORION ASCENDING

The car pulled onto the freeway. The family still had some time before they were to arrive at the distant campgrounds. The Professor explained, "We are right on schedule."

The weather was cooperating. The moon was about to set on the 21st of October.

This meteor shower is when the meteors seem to fall, radiate, or originate from, the constellation Orion.

Orion is the great hunter and warrior constellation which is quite easily found in the fall and winter night skies. His belt and sword help make it easily observable.

"What is a constellation?" Asked Alex?"

The Professor said, "A constellation is a word for con, connected, and stella, star. Constellations are connected stars.

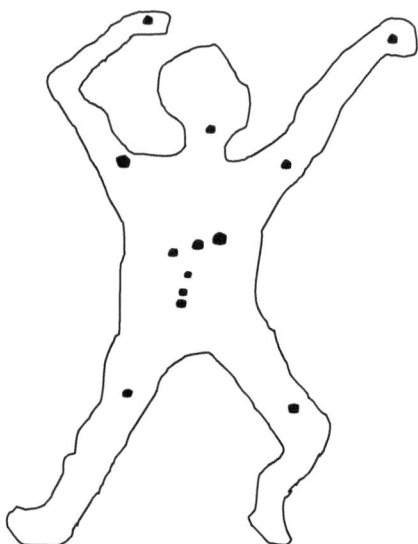

Long ago, people looked up at the sky and saw star patterns that seemed to form images. These groupings of connected stars are called constellations."

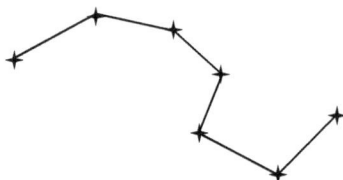

Mom drew Orion on one napkin, then the Big Dipper on another, "One familiar arrangement looks like a big dipper. We connect the stars together in our mind and it looks kind of like a big dipper. Maybe I should have brought more napkins!"

"Who can tell me why stars twinkle?" questioned Alexia.

Mom answered, "The moving layers of air and heat, warps, twists, and bends the light, making the stars appear to dance, shimmer, and twinkle."

The air that makes the stars twinkle, also protects the earth from most small meteors.

Meteors that reach the earth are called meteorites.

The effects of large meteorites probably destroyed the dinosaurs and many other creatures. It is estimated that the meteorite that probably killed the dinosaurs was most likely 11 or 12 kilometers wide, which is 7 or 8 miles in diameter, the size of a large city.

CHAPTER 5

BIRTHDAY SURPRISE!

EARTH

"Happy birthday. It's almost midnight, and tomorrow is your birthdays!" Mom remembered as she spoke to the twins. "You're both another year older. A year is the time it takes for the earth to travel once around the sun.

Each year, on your birthday, the stars appear in the night sky, in about the same position as on the day you were born! Your age tells you and others how many times you have been around the sun.

We add one day to the calendar every 4 years, to make up the extra day. It's called a leap day. It is added on February 29th. If you are born on February 29th you only have a birthday every 4 years!"

"That would be cool! I would never get old," Alex dreamed as he tried to see himself in the mirror.

"Why is it dark at night?" Asked Alexia.

"Well the earth rotates, turns, or spins like a moving toy top, on its axis, one time every day." Mom spun her finger around in the air. "As the sun shines on the Earth, one half is lit up, or day, and the other half is dark, or night. We are on the shaded dark side.

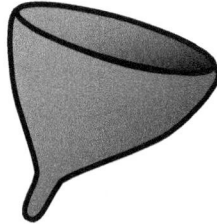

The sun seems to rise in the east, and then about 12 hours later, set in the west. But it is an illusion. That is not what is really happening. The sun does not move all day. It is the earth that is turning or spinning like a toy top. It appears that the sun moves across the sky, but really the earth is rotating smoothly and silently toward the east. The stars at night appear to do the same thing. They appear to rise in the east, and set about 12 hours later, in the west."

CHAPTER 6

ASTEROIDS, COMETS, AND METEORS, OH MY!

"What's the difference between an asteroid, comet, and a meteor?" asked Alexia.

Mom answered, "Asteroid comes from the word "aster" which means "a star" and "oid" which means likeness. Asteroids come from the asteroid belt. A region around the sun between Mars and Jupiter.

"Comets are made up of mostly dust and frozen ice," the Professor said. "Comets usually come from beyond Neptune's orbit, called the Kuiper belt. It is like a giant donut cloud."

"Did you bring the donuts and whipped cream?" Alex huffed. "I'm gettin' hungry; and you know how I like to eat!"

Alexia quickly wailed, "—and did we bring the marshmallows, graham crackers, and chocolate?"

Professor Jim continued, "As comets and asteroids travel around the sun, they leave behind long trails of fine dust—these are called swarms.

As the earth goes around the sun, it crosses the path of many swarms of different asteroids and comets throughout the year. The earth's air causes the meteor to burn white-hot as it leaves a streak of light across the night sky—called a meteor."

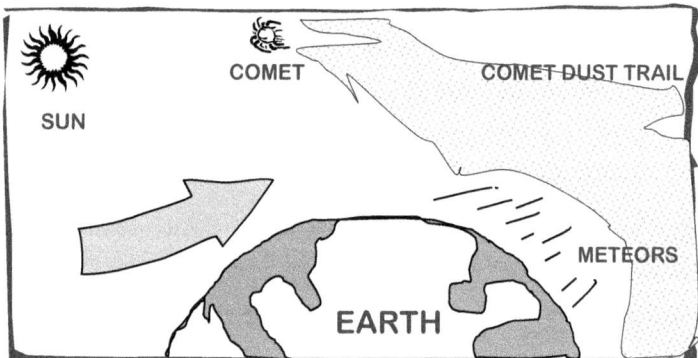

CHAPTER 7

THE FIREFLY ENCOUNTER

The car turned off the freeway and sped down the country road on its way to the campsite. The fields in the autumn night, were filled with glowing fireflies. The car plunged into a swarm of fireflies. Some had to give up their life for this adventure, as they hit the windshield.

"Look at all the glowing fireflies," Alexia commented with wonder in her eyes.

"Yes, and see all of the glowing streaks that they leave on the car's windshield," Alex grimaced and smiled at the same time.

Professor Jim rolled up his window, "The fireflies that hit our windshield are similar to the comet dust that hits the air around the earth.

The fireflies are not moving much; it is the car that is moving toward the fireflies.

The meteors are not moving much in the direction of the earth.

When you watch a meteor during a meteor shower, you are seeing an exclusive amazing event when everyone can see the earth moving through space at a fantastic speed.

You also get to see the direction the earth is moving. You are watching celestial mechanics work in real-time, as it happens!"

"Are celestial mechanics like guys who work on cars at night?" Alex joked, even though he wasn't sure what celestial mechanics were.

Professor Jim smiled as he replied, "It's the science of motion of heavenly bodies, due to gravity, through space. It's the awe-inspiring, silent, and amazing cosmic machine at work. It's similar to when you see a solar eclipse, when the moon passes in front of the sun, and blocks the sunlight.

A meteor shower is visual proof, observable evidence that the earth is rushing and hurtling silently through space, as it has for billions of years!

Your mother and father are your link to millions of your ancestors. You are the last survivor to carry on our hopes and dreams."

"What race are we in?" He added.

"The human race!" Spoke up Alexia.

"We are all brothers and sisters in the same family of humankind," Professor Jim spoke in a steady voice. "What is your skin color—white, black, red, or brown?"

"We are all shades of brown!" Chanted the children in unison. They had answered this question before.

Professor Jim continued, "No person is white or black. We are all individual shades of the same brown color! White is the color of snow—or the whites of your eyes. All pupils of the eye are black.

We are all the same in so many ways, living and surviving on the greatest planet in the whole Universe... our home... Earth!"

CHAPTER 8

THE CAMPSITE ARRIVAL

It was just before midnight when they arrived at the park. The weather was co-operating. The moon was about to set.

They saw a sign that read:

> METEOR SHOWER TONIGHT. MEET ON THE BIG MEADOW AT MIDNIGHT. WEATHER PERMITTING.

They pulled up to the dimly lit park entrance. The moonlight fell upon a familiar face. "Ranger Jerry!" Professor Jim exclaimed joyfully. "It is good to see you!"

Ranger Jerry taught the astronomy class at the park.

"Welcome, Professor Jim," smiled Jerry the park ranger, "I am glad to see you are back again this year. I think of you when I look up at the meteor showers and see that it is the earth moving up toward the meteors, not the meteors falling. You have changed the way I look at the world. I'm spreading the word of your discovery. Can I get you to autograph my hat?"

"Thanks Jerry, sure." As Jerry handed over his hat, Professor Jim got out the marker he usually carries, "It looks like great viewing tonight." He signed the bill of the ranger's hat, "And a good crowd turnout!"

"Enjoy your stay, and oh—there is another astrophysicist here tonight that would like to meet you. I'll introduce him to you later—if that is okay with you." Jerry said as he tipped his hat.

"I look forward to it. We'll be in the meadow." Professor Jim replied. They proceeded to their campsite.

The family quickly carried their gear to the large meadow. The twins opened up a tarp to keep the moisture off the sleeping bags. Mom and Dad set up their reclining lounge chairs on either side of the tarp. The twins tucked their sleeping bags between them.

There was enough tarp to pull up and cover most of the sleeping bags. This would keep the dew off overnight.

Occasionally, Professor Jim studied the heavens through his zoom binoculars.

No special equipment is needed to watch a meteor shower. Meteors travel so fast and far, that the meteor streaks only last about a second or less. They are best viewed with the naked eye. You may want to look at the awesome sight of the moon, planets, nebula, or other galaxies through binoculars or a telescope.

As Professor Jim started a bonfire, Alexia spoke up, "Quick, Dad," she said, "Let me borrow the binoculars before the crescent moon sets in the west."

After peering through the binoculars and taking a long pause, she added quietly, "I feel so small when I think of myself in the huge size of the Universe."

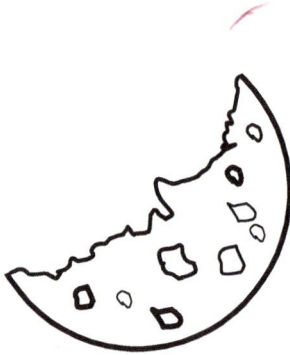

Night vision can take up to about 45 minutes to fully adapt and see your best in the dark. Do not look at bright lights, such as a bright moon, outdoor lights, car headlights, or cell phones. Use a red covered flashlight to maintain your night vision.

CHAPTER 9

EARTHLINGS TRAVEL AT FANTASTIC SPEED

As the family sat around the bonfire, Professor Jim repeated, "You know the earth we live on is going very quickly."

"Yes Dad, but how can we tell that we are moving as we go around the sun? I can't feel it," asked Alex with a puzzled look.

"No one can feel or hear the earth moving," Professor Jim continued, "Everything on the earth moves along with us as we go quickly, smoothly, and silently around the sun, one time each year.

We are all on a meteor adventure every minute of every day, but some people just do not know it yet!"

The earth is traveling much faster than any bullet, jet plane, or rocket.

Rifle bullets speed:

About 3,000 mph/4,800 kph

The fastest jets, the SR-71:

Over 2,100 mph/3,500 kph

The fastest manned rockets that travel to the space station:

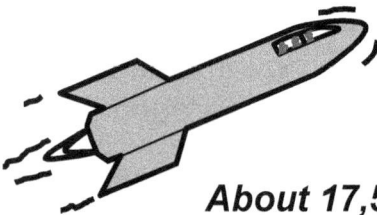

About 17,500 mph/28,000 kph

The earth is much faster:

Over 66,000 mph/106,000 kph

CHAPTER 10

GRAB YOUR SEAT AS YOU WATCH THE EARTH MOVE!

The sparks from the glowing timbers flew up like orange stars in the sky as the Professor threw another log on the raging bonfire.

"Wow, I just saw a meteor streak across the sky! I almost missed it!" Alex spoke with a loud whisper.

"Enjoy the show." The Professor tipped his chair back until it almost collapsed. "We ride together on a world called Terra Firma."

"Oh! There is another one. I can see that we are moving fast. It is breathtaking," Alexia voice started to quiver, "There are so many meteors! I want to go to the car, because I am worried and wondering if some may hit me."

Professor Jim assured her, "The meteors you see during a meteor shower are awesome, but the streaks of light are made from harmless dust particles smaller than a grain of sand. No one has ever been hit by a meteorite in recorded history. You are safe— and I have a big hug for you and the whole family!"

Everyone laughed as Caboose got in the middle of the group hug. He was one of the family.

The meteor shower outing brought the family together to see the magnificence of nature.

Mom said, "Meteor showers are mysterious and unpredictable. The suspense and anticipation is part of the pleasure. If you plan well, and are watchful, then you will have the thrill of seeing a meteor.

Some amateurs expect to see a huge down pouring of meteors each minute. Some viewers may become discouraged and give up watching. No one can exactly predict viewing conditions or meteor frequency."

"The dust burns very hot as the sky plunges into the dust." Alex poked at the fire.

As the family huddled around the roaring campfire to escape the night's chill, Professor Jim told the story of his original discovery.

"I've tried to see the big picture—to understand the world." I read the entire encyclopedia as a young teenager. I read every book on astronomy, physics, and science fiction in my school library. I would try to understand the motion of the earth, the seasons, and the planets' motion. I was curious and enjoyed reading. It has been said, 'fortune favors the well prepared mind,' Like a scout, try to be prepared for many things in your future. Learn from others and from books to understand and avoid many pitfalls. Reading with excellence at an early age is very important.

Don't let anyone tell you that you are not talented, gifted, and special. Believe in yourself. It gives you confidence and integrity. You are the most amazing thing in the known Universe! No one knows who or where the next great idea will come from. And one of the most amazing things to see on earth—is to see it moving through space. You know when you can see that!"

"Right Dad." groaned Alex with a smile. "We know."

"Keep the campfire burning," Professor Jim jumped up, "I'll be back in a bit—after I talk to those people over there with the Rangers."

"We know how you like to talk, Dad!" Alexia playfully teased as she cooked another marshmallow to perfection; then squeezed it and some chocolate between two graham crackers. "Do you want s'more before you go?" She giggled at her own play with words.

Professor Jim laughed, tipped his head back and looked up as he patted his stomach. Then he abruptly spun around and walked away, humming a tune.

"Why are meteors called shooting or falling stars?" asked Alex.

Mom answered, "Years ago, people thought stars were falling from the sky, as they saw a bright streak of light race across the night sky. But the stars are much farther away than the meteors and do not fall. Meteors may look like they are falling, but quite the opposite is true. The planet earth is going up toward the comet dust.

Some people make a wish upon a falling star. I wish that all your dreams come true!"

"How old are the stars?" asked Alexis.

Mom said, "It takes the light time to travel. Like the sound of an echo which takes a little time to return.

Light travels much quicker than sound. The light from our sun takes about 8 and ½ minutes to get to the earth. If the sun went dark now, no one on earth would know it for about 8 ½ minutes.

The light from the nearest star, not our sun, takes over 4 years to get here.

When we look at the stars, we are looking back in time at ancient stars."

"I've seen Uranus," shouted Professor Jim a little too loud as he returned to the party. "It takes 84 earth years for it to orbit the sun. I hope to live to see 84 times around the sun."

"How many times have you been around the sun, Dad?" Alex wrinkled his eyebrows.

"I have been around... quite a few," answered Professor Jim thoughtfully. "Quite a few..."

Mom laughed as she stirred the fire and blurted out, "That is one subject he doesn't want to talk about."

Alexia added, "And no Uranus jokes!"

THANKS MOM AND DAD, FOR TAKING US ON THIS METEOR ADVENTURE. LET'S DO THIS AGAIN SOON. I HAD A LOT OF FUN. CABOOSE LOOKS HAPPY TOO!

BOW-WOW BOW-WOW

It was a little before daybreak when Mom and Dad finally got to sleep. The smoke from the bonfire hung in the morning air. The fire's glowing embers were slowly going out.

The morning sunrise was brilliant as it lit up the meadow. The warming rays of the sun woke the family up.

As Alex put out the fire and finished off a big chunk of birthday cake he said, "Happy Birthday Sis'. This is one to remember!"

"Happy Birthday Bro'." she echoed.

They all agreed as they packed up their gear, that it was another successful star-gazing getaway.

Alex was thinking about what adventure would come his way next.

"I wonder…" said Alex with a smile, as they returned home, "If caboose will be ready for our next meteor adventure!"

PART TWO

FOR ADVANCED READERS

50

CHAPTER 11

FOR PRESENT AND FUTURE ASTRONOMERS, ASTROPHYSICISTS, AND STAR-GAZERS!

Introduce children to the night sky at an early age, if possible. It will likely be a night your children will remember for years. Enjoy your night out with the stars, nature, family, friends, and the Universe. Simple star-gazing can help you see your part in the great wonder of the vast Universe!

Throughout history, humankind has believed that meteors fall toward the earth. Now, people can realize the opposite is true; the earth moves toward the meteor dust during a meteor shower.

It is noteworthy that random meteors, not part of a meteor shower, do fall to earth due to the earth's gravitational pull.

This revolutionary discovery empowers people to visualize and experience our world from another viewpoint. This idea can change a person's perspective of the world.

You can better see the wider reality that we are all riding together on a little planet, compared to the cosmos. We are hurtling through infinite space, on our trip around the sun. The sun speeds around our galaxy which is called the Milky Way. It is called the Milky Way, because the stars are so far away, they look like milk.

CHAPTER 12

DISASTER

Many years ago, comets aroused many fears of poison gas, and evil spirits. The word disaster comes from "ill star," which implies great destruction, hardship, and loss of life. A comet would sometimes appear in the sky to look similar to a giant sword across the sky. This could influence a battle, or cause people to run and hide. Fear is usually caused when we do not understand something.

Today, they inspire wonder and awe. Comets can bring us information about the origin of the solar system, and from far away.

54

CHAPTER 13

SPEEDING THROUGH SPACE

We are traveling on the earth, at meteoric speed, over 66,000 miles an hour, which is over 106,000 kilometers per hour. This is 18 miles per second or 29 kilometers per second.

This speed amounts to over 584 million miles, which is 940 million kilometers traveled each year. Each year is 365¼ days.

Each day the earth travels over 1½ million miles, which is about 2½ million kilometers, on its trip around the sun.

The moon is also traveling along with the earth in its path around the sun.

The earth travels so fast, it goes the distance to the moon, in only four hours!

RADIANTS

Most meteor showers come out of, or radiate from, the spot in the night sky that the earth is moving towards.

Meteor showers seem to come from a specific area in the sky where the meteors seem to radiate from, called the radiant. Radiants are usually very close to the direction that the earth is traveling at the time you are seeing it. Many radiants seem to emanate or radiate from the ecliptic.

ECLIPTIC

The earth moves toward a region in the sky where the sun, moon, and planets travel. It is also where eclipses occur, called the ecliptic plane.

Where you are on the earth, the time of night, and the meteor's radiant, determines your best angle for viewing a meteor shower.

The earth is in an 'egg shaped' or elliptical path around the sun. On or around January 2-8th, the earth is closest to the sun, called perihelion. It is also when the earth is traveling at its fastest in its orbit.

THE EARTH'S YEARLY TRAVELS

The stars appear to rise in the east and set in the west, but it is actually the rotation of the earth.

The stars in the night sky also appear to have an additional movement. If you watch the stars for a few weeks at the same time every night, each night the stars would appear to drift west. As the months go by, the stars appear to move west until one year later they return to their original position.

What is really happening, is that the earth is moving eastwardly, in its huge path around the sun. The stars are so far away, that they appear to be mostly stationary. The earth moves in a complete circle under the stars, to return to the same position each year on the same day.

COMET DUST

Each comet and asteroid varies in its direction and speed in its path around the sun. The dust and gas which trails an asteroid or comet can cause slight variations in the meteors apparent or origin of the radiant.

Comet dust also goes around the sun, but in a different path and speed than the earth.

Many comet dust trails have little effective speed in the direction of the earth.

The earth's rotation, increased air density, and gravity, have very little observable effect on the meteor dust, during a meteor shower.

Comet dust trails vary in angle, speed, and direction, which can shift some radiants from the ecliptic plane.

This is like driving in a cross wind through a swarm of fireflies. The fireflies' origin would appear to shift from the center of the windshield.

Each comet or asteroid can create enough dust such that a meteor shower can last several days.

THIS IS ASTROPHYSICIST APPROVED

This discovery of visual proof, was sought throughout history, right up to today. The search went on from the genius of Aristarchus, the ancient astronomer, to Nicolas Copernicus, Johannes Kepler, Galileo Galilei, and Isaac Newton, right up to the greatest astronomers and astrophysicists of modern day.

This new revelation of astronomical phenomena, was discovered in December 2004, by Professor James Pressler, Ph.D.

This exclusive discovery is the only visual proof that the earth is going around the sun, without using a telescope or any other special equipment.

This visual proof substantiates the hypothesis and is additional direct empirical evidence, confirmed by observation that the earth goes around the sun.

You can see visual proof of the 66,000 mile per hour or 107,000 kilometers per hour, speed of the earth as it orbits the sun. The mystery of planetary motion through the cosmos is now reaffirmed and can be plainly witnessed by an observer, without special equipment. You can see celestial mechanics as it is happening, in real time! The observation of the peak rate per hour of each meteor shower will appear to repeat on, or about the same night, every year.

The theory that the earth orbits the sun is strongly supported by other direct empirical evidence called "stellar parallax" and the "aberration of starlight."

Stellar parallax is seen when 2 photographs, taken 6 months apart, are compared. The nearer stars will appear to change position from the much farther background stars. Like a pencil, held at arm's length. It will seem to change position when seen from the left or right eye.

Stellar aberration, happens when a telescope's incoming starlight, as seen from the moving earth, causes the apparent position of the star to differ slightly from its true position.

Stellar aberration is like when a person runs through the rain with an umbrella. The runner has to tip the umbrella forward to deflect the rain.

We are traveling at meteoric speed as we go around the sun, and plunge into the comet's dust trails, called swarms. We are all on a meteor adventure as we ride on the earth! We can watch the speed and direction of our adventure as we see the streaks of glowing white hot dust when it hits our upper air and burns up. The meteor dust reaches temperatures of around 3,000° Fahrenheit. Which is over 1600° Celsius.

Meteor showers are unpredictable. How many will appear to fall depends on many variables: the comet's path, the earth's position, your location and viewing conditions, the viewer's eyesight, the moon's intensity, and other factors.

After midnight, is when the sky we are watching is turned to the direction that the earth is moving, while traveling around the sun.

A meteor shower will peak in number of trails of light or streaks of light across the night sky. It will happen again next year on or around the same day. This reappearance each year on the same day, is visual proof and reaffirms that the earth is going around the sun.

CHAPTER 14

MAJOR METEOR SHOWERS

Dates	Shower	Peak Date Near	Rate Per Hour
Jan 1-5	Quadrantids	Jan 3	30-200
Apr 16-25	Lyrids	Apr 22	8-100
Apr 19-May 28	Eta Aquarids	May 5	10-50
Jul 21-Aug 23	Delta Aquarids	Jul 28	15-20
Jul 13-Aug 26	Perseids	Aug 12	50-200
Oct 4-Nov 14	Orionid's	Oct 21	7-35
Nov 4-13	Taurids	Nov 5	8-10
Nov 5-30	Leonids	Nov 17	10-4000
Dec 4-16	Geminids	Dec 13	50-100
Dec 17-25	Ursids	Dec 19	5-20

Activity dates & rates can vary from year to year.

Meteor showers span a range of dates. The day before and the day after a peak shower event may be good, as well.

The Leonids meteor shower, which the radiant appears to originate from the constellation Leo, the lion, was discovered by Temple-Tuttle. It returns every 33 years.

Leonids Meteor Shower, which peaks in November, can sometimes leave meteor trains of a glowing streak of golden light.

A meteor train is the smoke or light trail left behind the meteor. They are rare, unpredictable, and marvelous to observe.

HOW OLD WILL YOU BE WHEN HALLEY'S COMET RETURNS IN THE YEAR 2061?

The Orionid Meteor Shower peaks around October 21. It occurs when the earth passes through the dust left behind from Halley's Comet. Halley's Comet is on its way back from the sun to beyond the planet Neptune. Its journey takes 76 years to orbit the sun on its big oval, or ellipse. Edmund Halley discovered in 1705 that the same comet can be seen over and over again. He predicted its return. The comet showed up just like he predicted. That is why it is named in his behalf—Halley's Comet. Edmond Halley was the first discoverer to understand that some comets return on a regular cycle.

The comet named after him was first recorded in the year 467, it was last seen in 1986. Its next showing will be in 2061. Edmond Halley's discovery was the first direct confirmation of Isaac Newton's theory of universal gravitation.

We can see when the earth passes thru the Halley's Comet dust trail. The Orionid's shower, which appears from the Orion constellation in October, is the dust trail from the incoming comet. In May, the earth crosses the outbound trail called Eta Aquarid's, which has been left behind by the famous Halley's Comet.

CHAPTER 15

RECORD YOUR METEOR SHOWER ACTIVITY

WRITE DOWN AND LOG:
- Your location and sky conditions.
- Date, time, length, and duration of each meteor.
- Color and brightness.
- Number of meteors per hour.
- Length and duration of the meteor train.
- Indicate the radiant, the area where the meteors seem to originate.

An exclamation point could have originated from the shape of a meteor, or comet.

During a meteor shower, when you see a meteor burn for one second, you are seeing the earth move about 29 kilometers, which is about 18 miles, which is about the speed of the earth!

Our whole solar system is called the heliosphere. The heliosphere encompasses the sun, the planets, the comets and asteroids, and all the dust and gas that surrounds and orbits the sun. Our solar system is also traveling around the galaxy at over three times as fast as the earth is moving around the sun! And our galaxy is traveling around other galaxies even faster!

WHERE ARE YOU FROM?

You were formed from the atoms and elements from within ancient stars that collapsed and exploded. We are made from ancient stardust. We are a part of the heavens. We are heavenly, powerful, and glorious.

The Universe has created you—your parents have given you your life and your name.

You were created from your mother and father and millions of your ancestors.

Keep in mind that we are all together, riding as one family of humankind, on this giant spaceship earth as you see it speed around the sun!

FOR FURTHER RESEARCH, GO TO:
http//:www.iread-edu.com

YOUR FRIEND,
THE END...For now.

Look for our next books and videos, coming soon to a computer, phone, or printing press near you.

WHEN EVERY PAGE HAS A STAR,
OR YOU GET A STAR FOR READING SO FAR,
YOU ARE GOING TO GO FAR
PUT A BIG STAR IN THE BAR,
OR DOWNLOAD ONE, MAYBE FROM YOUR CAR,
AWARD YOURSELF A SUPER STAR!

Explore your imagination and enrich your powers of observation and inquiring mind with the power and freedom of advanced reading ability.

Don't forget to write!

ABOUT THE AUTHOR AND ILLUSTRATOR

PROFESSOR Jim Pressler Ph.D., born in Dearborn Michigan, has traveled most of the United States, Europe and the Middle East and promotes childhood literacy. *Professor Jim* bought his first large telescope at age 12. He enjoys camping and stargazing with his sons. He also has a fascination with steam trains and custom cars. *Professor Jim* believes he has a dream job. He makes dreams come true. Through academic excellence, a child can succeed in the endeavors they pursue.

This story was inspired by real life experiences. The dog named Caboose in the story was rescued from an animal shelter.

Caboose was rescued from an animal shelter. Your thoughts are bright, and don't forget to write! Your friend...   The end.

PROFESSOR JIM is the owner and director of the *iREAD ACADEMY,* which offer excellence in reading, math, and writing.

Professor Jim is the author of several books and videos. He can be contacted at:
jimxpressler@yahoo.com
http//:www.iread-edu.com

Look for these three books in the *iREAD ACADEMY* COLLECTION

THE SKILL OF READING/CHILDHOOD TO ADULT EDUCATION
HANDBOOK 1: BEGINNING READING ESSENTIALS
HANDBOOK 2: ADVANCED READING EXCELLENCE

ACADEMIC SUCCESS READING SYSTEM –

**WE ARE AT THE FOREFRONT OF THE GREATEST ERA OF
LEARNING IN HISTORY. MAKE SURE YOUR STUDENT
KNOWS THESE ESSENTIALS TO EXCELLENCE. IT IS THE
FINEST GIFT & SKILL YOU CAN GIVE THEM.**
These two handbooks quickly and simply train readers how to
read, understand math fundamentals, and writing with excellence
and confidence. Required reading for students who want to
succeed academically. Quickly unlock the secrets of the ages,
and gain a deeper understanding of the books of knowledge; as
well as those who want to treat and cure to escape their reading
deficits or struggles, such as dyslexia, ADD, or Gifted/Talented.

**A BREAKTHROUGH IN TEACHING READING YOU CANNOT
GET ANYWHERE ELSE.**

This "RIMER PRIMER" complete guided reading system, uses
over 100 rhyming word families, riddles and word games to
make it enjoyable and interesting for the instructor and student.
This cooperative teaching method motivates a student, in an
easy to read step-by-step method, without jargon, or diacritical
marks. Many of the reading secrets revealed in this reading
system have been lost or unused for over 2,600 years.

**THIS INSPIRING METHOD IS THE KEY TO UNLOCKING
THE SECRETS OF THE READING CODE.** This reading
system is a paragon of learning. Feel the satisfaction and joy of
passing on the greatest skill ever developed to transfer
knowledge; -the magical ability to read the written word.

Professor Jim's BEGINNING READING ADVENTURES

**FAT
CAT
AT
BAT**

VAT

READING ESSENTIALS HANDBOOK OF KNOWLEDGE

THE ESSENTIALS TO ACADEMIC SUCCESS, FROM BEGINNING TO ADVANCED READING SYSTEM. AGES 4-ADULT. Includes *Professor Jim's* discovery of the origin of the alphabet.

PROFESSOR JIM PRESSLER, Ph.D.
READING SPECIALIST, ASTRONOMER

Professor Jim's **AMAZING
READING ADVENTURE SERIES:**
"ESSENTIALS TO EXCELLENCE"
RIMER PRIMER

**HANDBOOK 1
FUN RIMES**

iREAD ACADEMY
THE CENTER FOR THE TREATMENT OF READING DISORDERS, AND ADVANCED READING, WRITING, AND MATH TECHNIQUES.

ISBN-13: 978-0-9788828-0-8

THIS HANDBOOK IS EXPRESSLY FOR:

NAME: _____

Professor Jim's

ADVANCED READING ADVENTURES
WITH WRITING, MATH, AND RIMES AND SIGNS FOR SAFETY.

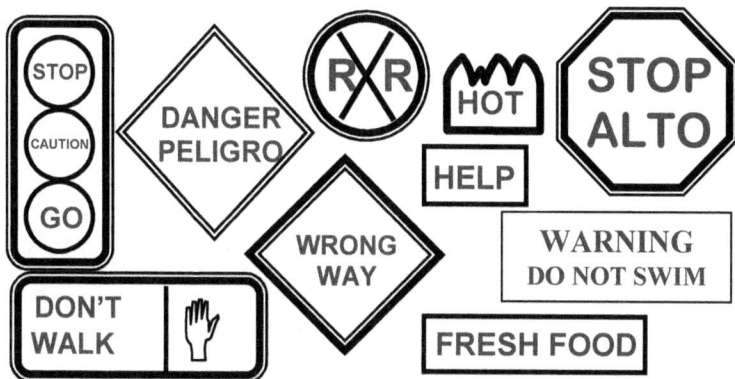

Good readers can be safer, more self-confident, and improve their success in education and quality of life. This handbook series teaches the skill of reading quickly, simply, and effectively. AGES 4-ADULT SCHOLARS

PROFESSOR JIM PRESSLER, Ph.D.
READING SPECIALIST, ASTRONOMER

Professor Jim's AMAZING
READING ADVENTURE Series:
"ESSENTIALS TO EXCELLENCE"

HANDBOOK 2
ADVANCED

iREAD ACADEMY
THE CENTER FOR THE TREATMENT OF READING DISORDERS, AND ADVANCED READING, WRITING, AND MATH TECHNIQUES.

ISBN-13: 978-0-9788828-4-6

THIS HANDBOOK IS EXPRESSLY FOR:

NAME: _____

Professor Jim's
WISDOM FOR SAGES OF ALL AGES!
A children's epic rime where their dreams can pass the time.   An inspiring nighttime rime to encourage reading adventures!

LOOK FOR THESE AND OTHER PRODUCTS AT:

www.iread-edu.com
GET ON THE FAST TRACK OF LEARNING

If you like this reading program and the effort to help children read with excellence, please tell your friends.

If you like this book, please leave a simple book review when finished if possible. We are constantly trying to improve and your opinion is appreciated. Thank You.